50
WAYS TO
GREENER
TRAVEL

SIÂN BERRY

ABOUT
THE AUTHOR

Siân Berry is the Green Party's candidate for London Mayor in 2008 and is a founder of the successful campaign group, the Alliance Against Urban 4x4s.

Siân was one of the Green Party's Principal Speakers until September 2007 and was previously national Campaigns Co-ordinator. She stood in the Hampstead and Highgate constituency in the 2005 General Election and has campaigned in her local area for more affordable housing and, nationally, to promote renewable energy and local shops.

Famous for the mock parking tickets created by Siân in 2003, the Alliance Against Urban 4x4s is now a national campaign and the group recently celebrated persuading the current Mayor of London to propose a higher congestion charge for big 4x4 vehicles and other gas-guzzlers.

Siân studied engineering at university and her professional background is in communications. These skills give her a straightforward and accessible approach to promoting green issues, focusing on what people can do today to make a difference, and on what governments need to do to make greener lives easier for everyone.

As spokesperson for the Alliance and a well-known Green Party figure, Siân has received wide coverage in national and international newspapers and has appeared on numerous TV and radio shows, from Radio 4's *Today* programme to *Richard and Judy*. Her calm, cheerful and persuasive advocacy has stimulated a lively public debate about 4x4s, and has helped to raise the environment further up the public agenda.

50
WAYS TO
GREENER
TRAVEL

SIÂN BERRY

Kyle Cathie Ltd

First published in Great Britain in 2008 by
Kyle Cathie Ltd
122 Arlington Road, London NW1 7HP
general.enquiries@kyle-cathie.com
www.kylecathie.com

10 9 8 7 6 5 4 3 2 1

978-1-85626-775-5

Editorial Director: Muna Reyal
Illustrator and Designer: Aaron Blecha
Production Director: Sha Huxtable

A Cataloguing In Publication record for this title is
available from the British Library.

Colour reproduction by Scanhouse
Printed and bound in Italy by Amadeus

Printed on 100% recycled paper

**THE CIVILIZED MAN
HAS BUILT A COACH,
BUT HAS LOST THE
USE OF HIS FEET.**

Ralph Waldo Emerson

50 WAYS TO...

In the home, in the garden, at the shops, at work and on the move, this series of books contains a wide range of simple ways to live a greener life, whatever your situation. Each book has fifty easy, affordable and creative tips to help you live more lightly on the planet.

There are many ways to be green that don't need a big investment of money, time, effort or space. Saving energy also saves money on your bills, and eco-friendly products don't have to be high-tech and expensive.

Any size garden – or even a window box – can be a haven for wildlife and provide useful low-maintenance crops that save on imported fruit and vegetables. And those of us living in towns and cities should know that urban living can provide some of the lowest-carbon lifestyles around.

The 50 Ways series has been written by Siân Berry: Green Party candidate for Mayor of London in 2008 and a founder of the successful campaign group the Alliance Against Urban 4x4s. She shares her experiences to demonstrate how you can reduce your carbon footprint, stay ahead of fashion and enjoy life without sacrifice.

Siân says: 'Being green is not about giving everything up; it's about using things cleverly and creatively to cut out waste. In these books, I aim to show you that a greener life without fuss is available to everyone'.

INTRODUCTION

The travel choices we make have a big impact on the contribution we make to climate change. Around a quarter of our carbon footprint is created by personal travel and, unlike for other activities, emissions from transport are going up, not down. We need to turn this trend around quickly if we don't want to cancel out all our other efforts to save the planet.

Every powered method of transport is responsible for putting carbon dioxide into the atmosphere, but the amount varies hugely – from just nine grams per kilometre for a long-distance coach to more than 500 grams per kilometre for some short-haul airline tickets. And, of course, there are lots of human-powered, virtually carbon-free methods of travel, including walking and cycling.

This book aims to put our travel choices in context. We can do a lot to reduce our carbon emissions simply by being cleverer about when and where we travel. By combining trips and sharing lifts, we can get the same amount done, but reduce the number of journeys we take in the process.

For day-to-day travel, most of us still rely on the car, even for very short journeys, so plenty of the advice in this book covers alternatives to the car for trips we make on a regular basis: to school, to work and to the shops.

Reducing the amount of traffic on our streets isn't just a good thing to do because of carbon dioxide. Towns and cities with fewer cars clogging up roads will also enjoy improved air quality, safer streets where children can play, and better local economies with thriving local shops and businesses.

For longer trips and holidays, growth in air travel is the main threat to reducing our carbon emissions, so here you can also read about the joys of holidaying close to home and about exploring the world in more enjoyable and more sustainable ways.

I hope this book inspires you to try a wider range of transport options and gives you lots of ideas for greener ways to get about.

WALKING BACK
TO HAPPINESS

We are walking less and less, and in the process getting more overweight every year.

There's a lot of talk about our obesity epidemic, and we tend to assume this is all down to eating more. However, several studies have found that the average number of calories eaten has gone down since the 1970s, so a more important factor is the reduction in daily exercise, thanks to our habit of getting into the car even for very short journeys.

A quarter of all car trips cover distances that could be walked instead. People who drive regularly walk about an hour a week less than people without a car in the driveway – a total of 200 kilometres (124 miles) less on average per year. All those calories not burned really do add up; over ten years this 'walking deficit' could lead to a weight gain of thirteen kilograms!

Our car culture reinforces itself and reduces the chances we all get to walk. Housing estates and shopping centres are planned with car drivers in mind, increasing the distances we need to travel to find essential services, making sure that walking declines even further.

We can learn a lot from our parents and grandparents. In their youth, they were far more active than we are today. The average energy used up in the course of a day has gone down by about 800 calories since the 1940s, thanks to fewer manual jobs, a huge rise in car ownership and the need to travel further to work or shop, leading to a reliance on four wheels rather than two legs.

Walking more can help with so many problems, and incorporating more walking into our daily routines can be very simple. Follow these tips to build up your health as well as cut down on your carbon footprint.

1 WALK TO BE SLIM AND FIT

To be fit and healthy, we should be physically active, but most of us don't move about nearly enough. A healthy distance to walk is about 10,000 steps per day, but people in sit-down jobs who drive to work only average around 3,000.

It's very easy to build short walking trips into your daily routine, whether it's a trip to the local shops or taking public transport instead of the car on a longer journey to work or a night out. Even people in low-activity jobs increase their total to about 7,000 steps if they use the bus or train, thanks to that walk to the station or bus stop.

I certainly noticed this effect when I was borrowing my dad's car to get to work. Without eating any more than usual, I steadily put on weight and resorted to a strict diet that wasn't any fun at all – all because I was no longer walking half a mile to the bus stop. Nowadays, I walk regularly and use public transport or my bike to get to work, and can enjoy a pudding every now and again without worrying about bursting out of my clothes.

Walking is a great way to keep at a healthy weight if you don't want to worry about what to eat. Studies in the USA have shown that each extra kilometre walked per day leads to nearly a 5 per cent reduction in the chances of becoming obese, whereas each extra hour spent in the car increases this risk by about 6 per cent.

2 WALK TO THINK

I wasn't surprised to find out that walking is a proven cure for stress – it's thought that the rhythmic movements and the leisurely pace of the world going by are what helps to improve mental wellbeing in people who take long walks on a regular basis.

Walking can bring inspiration, too. Many great writers, including Charles Dickens and William Wordsworth, did a lot of their thinking while taking walks. All his life, from going to work in a factory in his youth to when he was Britain's most famous author, Dickens walked for miles at a time through the streets of London, observing city life and getting ideas for characters and situations to include in his stories.

Wordsworth spent much of his time in the Lake District in England, where he walked daily in the hills, drawing inspiration for his work and composing poems before putting them down on paper when he got home.

Even if you are not planning to create great works of art, walking is a great way to clear away stress during the working day. People who walk on the way to work or go for a stroll at lunchtime report that they feel more alert and think more clearly as a result.

WALK TO
THE SHOPS 3

The distance the average person travels to go shopping has increased over the last two decades from around 300 miles a year to nearly 450 miles a year. At the same time, we're taking fewer and fewer of these journeys on foot, because local shops are closing and the distance for each shopping trip increases.

Walking to the shops is a great way to put more walking into your everyday life. We know that shopping locally can help cut down on car journeys and those steps to the local shops will help your general fitness as well, especially if you are carrying shopping.

For shops that are further away, why not take the opportunity to enjoy a walk into town and then get a bus or taxi home with your shopping afterwards? I often do this in London: walking to the high street in the next borough and then catching the bus or tube home again when I have heavy bags.

4 WALK TO WORK

The key to turning walking into a regular habit is to make it second nature rather than an 'extra' thing that you will give up after a few goes. So, the daily journey into work is an ideal trip to switch to an active, walking journey.

As with most trips, we are walking to work less than ever; in the last 30 years, the proportion of people travelling to work on foot has halved. Unfortunately, the cost of housing, and the way workplaces cluster away from residential areas mean that many of us live too far from work to make the whole journey possible on foot.

However, the benefits of a brisk early morning walk to clear your head, get the blood flowing and set you up for the day are so great that it's worth building walking into your trip to work in any way you can.

Many public transport journeys involve catching a train to a main transport hub and then a local bus to the office. If your journey is like this, why not try walking instead of catching the bus on the last leg of the trip? By not relying on two sets of public transport to get you to work on time, you can take some of the uncertainty out of the journey, and arrive at work feeling healthier and happier.

You could also try taking a bus that you've ignored before because it doesn't go directly to the door of your workplace. If you are happy to walk the last bit, other routes may be just as suitable – and being flexible also gives you more options on mornings when there are problems with the service.

5 WALK UP THE STAIRS

While any steps we take in the course of the day will contribute to reaching our healthy 10,000 steps target, walking up stairs has the added benefit of being real exercise.

Doctors have found that, to benefit our hearts, we should do 30 minutes of moderate exercise five times a week. Moderate exercise is defined as activities strenuous enough to increase our breathing rate and heart rate, and walking up a few flights of stairs several times a day certainly qualifies as strenuous enough. Once you notice it getting easier, you'll know it's doing you good.

Other everyday tasks also involve moderate exercise, so to stay healthy you should never need to join a gym. Volunteer to do the vacuuming, mow the lawn or catch up on DIY tasks around the home. These all raise the heart rate enough to give real health benefits, and after doing these activities, you're less likely to want to undo the good work by rewarding yourself with a sugary snack than if you made a special trip to the gym.

WALK TO THE VIEW 6

Once we are fit and healthy enough to climb a few flights of stairs without needing half an hour to get our breath back, walking for further and longer for fun is one of the best leisure activities around.

More than eight million people in the UK take regular leisure walks. Walking for pleasure is our second favourite thing to do with our spare time, after eating out and eating in with family and friends.

We enjoy it because we love the feeling of the wind on our faces and the satisfaction of reaching the summit of a hill or mountain and sitting down to enjoy a well-earned view. I live near a hill with a fantastic view over London and, at the weekend, it's packed with people striding up to get some fresh air. On Christmas Day, it's busier than the motorway as everyone walks off that big dinner.

If you're keen to try rambling but don't know where to start, it's easy to find guides to walks in your area in local bookshops, and there are plenty of published books covering everything from pub walks to routes that integrate well with trains and buses. Your local tourist information service is likely to have guides for visitors showing the best routes that take in local attractions and views, and the Ramblers' Association has a wide range of literature on the subject, and organises guided walks all over the country.

THE FREEDOM
OF TWO WHEELS

Cycling is easily the most energy-efficient way of getting around – far ahead of walking as the lowest energy user per kilometre. This is because it employs eco-friendly human power in a very efficient way, using up fewer calories than walking by up to five times.

In a car, the equivalent of one hundred calories of fuel energy will take you less than 300 feet along the road, but on a bike, the same amount of energy from food will take you around three miles.

The bicycle, with its simple levers, gears and wheels, is so clever it was voted the best invention ever made in a poll a couple of years ago, easily beating the computer and the electric motor.

Cities that make cycling easy see the benefits for their citizens. In Copenhagen, a third of people cycle to work, not just because they want to save the planet, but because it's faster and easier than public transport or the car. The city has excellent cycle lanes, lots of parking spots, and even free bikes available for a small deposit – a scheme now being brought to Paris and London because it works so well.

This all sounds like cycling heaven, but even if your town or city doesn't do as much for bikes as Copenhagen, travelling on two wheels still has lots of plus points: improving health and fitness while saving you money and time.

You don't have to become 'a cyclist' or join a club, and daily commuting may not be for you (until your company brings in decent parking and showers). However, there are lots of journeys for which a bike is by far the best way to travel, and every journey helps the climate and your fitness as well.

7 CYCLE TO SAVE TIME

With traffic in London and other cities still grinding along at the average speed of a horse and carriage, bicycles are actually the quickest way to travel. On a bike, you spend around 90 per cent of the time on the move, and because it is also a door-to-door form of transport, every study finds that cycling is the fastest way of making a short, urban journey.

The figures show that any journey of less than two miles is best done by bike and, for distances of up to five miles, a bike can still beat the car at busy times.

One of the best things about cycling to work is its predictability. Unlike cars and buses, which are at the mercy of traffic jams and other delays, bike trips take almost exactly the same amount of time every day. This means that, on your bike, you don't have to allow extra time in case of problems and you can be much more certain of reaching your destination on schedule.

8 CYCLE FOR HEALTH

Cycling uses 300 to 1,000 calories per hour, depending on your speed and the number of hills, so it is a great way to lose weight and get healthy.

The health benefits of cycling have been well studied. The long list of diseases regular cycling helps to avoid amazed even me when I did my research. Overall, cyclists have around a third lower risk of death compared with non-cyclists, have much lower levels of obesity, and the level of fitness of someone five to ten years younger!

Cycling regularly helps reduce your risk of:
- heart disease
- many cancers
- diabetes
- bad cholesterol levels
- sleep problems

and helps promote:
- weight loss
- fitness and strength
- tolerance to stress

So, a bike is one of the best 'medicines' around, with very few side effects. With all this to gain, there's no reason to put off getting that bike out of the garage any longer!

CYCLE SAFELY 9

Some people worry about their safety on a bike, but the perception of danger is not based on any real evidence. Cycling is actually safer than walking and just as safe as being in a car for a short journey. Overall, in terms of life expectancy, the benefits of cycling outweigh any risks by a factor of more than twenty.

There's also safety in numbers, which every new bike on the road helps to increase. With more bikes, you might expect more accidents, but, in fact, the more cyclists there are, the more car drivers notice and look out for them, so the safer it gets. In London, an 83 per cent increase in cycling since 2000 has been accompanied by a 28 per cent reduction in cyclists killed and injured.

The best way to improve your safety (assuming you are already wearing a helmet) is to ride with confidence. A few hours' training is a good idea if you feel you need it, and there are organisations offering classes and accompanied rides for adults listed at the back of this book.

10 TIPS FOR HAPPY CYCLING

Follow these simple tips and you'll be a safe, happy and confident bike user in no time.

Get into the right position

Take the space you are entitled to on the road. Ride at least a metre away from the kerb and parked cars. Giving yourself room means that passing vehicles will also give you more space and you'll be much safer than if you squeeze into the edge of the road, where you are also more likely to find bumps and debris that could damage your tyres.

Be visible

Wear bright colours and, especially at night, reflective strips or a high-visibility vest. Make sure you use lights in the dark, and decorate your bike with reflective strips, including its sides. Most accidents occur because drivers haven't noticed a bike approaching, so give them no excuse to miss you.

Keep your eyes and ears open

The best defence is to spot danger early, so stay alert while cycling and avoid listening to music through headphones.

Expect the unexpected

Dangers may not spot you, but by anticipating problems, you give yourself time to react and get yourself out of trouble.

Top unexpected hazards include car doors being opened, pedestrians stepping out into the road, drivers who don't indicate before turning, and cars creeping out of side roads. Give this last hazard lots of room, as drivers trying to join a road often don't notice cyclists and may pull forwards without warning.

Take extra care at junctions

Most accidents involving cyclists take place at junctions. Lorries turning across your path are the biggest danger, so never get caught between a big vehicle and the kerb at the traffic lights. Get to the front of the queue and then wait in the centre of the lane to set off.

If you are moving up a row of stationary traffic towards a red signal, make sure you have time to reach the front before the lights turn green. If not, wait behind any lorries and let them go first.

Stay calm and polite

If drivers don't respect you, it can be tempting to break the rules yourself. Resist this temptation and always be a good example of a calm and friendly cyclist. Catch a driver's eye at a junction, make your direction clear, and they will respect your right to be on the road. If someone is rude, simply smile. Remember, you'll probably get to your destination quicker than they will!

BEST JOURNEYS BY BIKE

If you're not ready to be a full-time commuting cyclist, start by replacing just some of your journeys with a bike ride. These journeys are ideal for the part-time cyclist to make on two wheels.

To the gym

A bike is as good as the gym to keep you fit (it even pays you to join by saving you money), but many people still drive to their gym and then get on an exercise bike. Stop this madness by cycling there instead. You'll be able to reduce your time spent working out, and spend more time in the swimming pool or sauna instead.

To the shops

Get a basket or pannier and cycle to your local shops to combine fitness with saving the planet, cutting down on waste and supporting your local community. How many other activities bring that many benefits at once?

To the train

Any journey less than two miles long is an ideal bike journey.
If you are commuting by car because the train station is too far
away, taking the bike to the train can be the perfect combination.

Lots of trains will take full-size bikes, but some of the best bikes
to use in combination with public transport are compact folding
models. I have one of these and it's really flexible. I sometimes
take it on the bus when it's raining and it folds up so small I don't
have to lock it up outside people's houses but can take it into the
hallway. I've even taken it into pubs and restaurants and kept it
under the table without raising any eyebrows.

CUTTING DOWN ON CAR JOURNEYS

Car journeys are surprisingly easy to cut down on when people have a real incentive. Extraordinary events, such as earthquakes, sometimes mean whole roads or bridges are closed for long periods of time and, in these circumstances, what almost always happens is that, instead of all those cars clogging up other routes, many journeys simply 'evaporate' and don't take place at all.

When London brought in a charge for vehicles entering the centre of town, local newspapers predicted that thousands of cars would switch to roads surrounding the area and cause huge problems. But, instead of traffic chaos, what happened was that traffic inside the charging zone went down, and the number of cars on surrounding roads stayed much the same. People were left wondering where the cars went!

The fact is, when people know that roads aren't available or will cost them money to travel on, they almost unconsciously make different decisions about how, when and whether to travel. They may combine several journeys into one, share a lift with someone else, travel at a less busy time, or simply decide not to go somewhere they think will mean sitting in a traffic jam.

There may not be a major disaster closing roads in your town, but climate change is a potential disaster that means journeys are definitely worth avoiding where possible. Using the same kinds of ideas as people do after an earthquake, we can make a real difference by using a range of methods to cut down painlessly on the number of car journeys we make.

12 COMBINE YOUR TRIPS INTO ONE

Do you ever have days when you feel like a one-person taxi service? You get home from a trip to town, then immediately have to go out again to ferry the kids to football training or take something round to grandma's house. When you're doing up your kitchen or bathroom, do you find yourself going back to the shops several times to get extra bits and pieces you didn't realise you needed on the last trip?

All these never-ending car trips is not just a waste of carbon emissions, but also a waste of your time, especially when many of these separate journeys could be combined into one.

The answer is simply to plan ahead. Ask the kids what they're up to this weekend, then plan your other trips around them – better still, put them on the bus! Make a proper list before you go to the shops and you'll get some of your weekend back, as well as lots of green brownie points.

SHARE
A LIFT

3

Lots of car journeys are taken by large groups of people all going to the same place, such as a sporting event, a concert or a workplace.

Another very simple way to cut your per-person emissions is to share a lift with someone else who is going to the same place. You'd probably jump at the chance to buy a green car which achieved twice the mileage of your current model, but by sharing a car, you can already cut your per-person emissions in half.

With four in the car, you'll end up with the same emissions as if each of you was making the journey in a super-efficient hybrid: four people sharing a small car that emits 140 grams per kilometre works out at just 35 grams per kilometre each.

Organising lift-sharing with friends is as easy as making a phone call, and lift-sharing for work can be organised as part of a workplace travel plan (see later). For trips you aren't making to work or with friends, a good way to find travel buddies is to use a service such as the Liftshare website. This helps people to find travelling companions for regular trips and occasional journeys. And because everyone is registered by the site, you have added security and peace of mind.

14 JOIN A CAR CLUB

Joining a car club can save you money and help you reduce your impact on the environment without giving up all the benefits of a car.

In a car club, vehicles are shared between local members. After joining the club, you simply book by telephone or on a website, and then use your electronic membership card and pin number to unlock and drive one of the cars (which are parked in dedicated spaces around the country). You pay a joining fee and then an hourly rate to use a car.

People in car clubs drive 60–70 per cent fewer miles than people who own a car but with no reduction in quality of life as a result. This is a classic example of journey 'evaporation'; car club members still have a car whenever they want it and booking only takes a few minutes, but this short delay still means they are naturally encouraged to combine trips and use other methods of transport when they are easier.

There are many other benefits of car clubs:

• Each car replaces around six private cars, so they reduce the amount of car parking cluttering up the streets.

• Because club cars are generally newer and less polluting than the average car, big carbon dioxide reductions are possible. Users of the car club in San Francisco have reduced their personal emissions by 2.3 tonnes each.

• Most members save a lot of money. If you drive less than 6,000 miles per year (about 75 per cent of the average), joining a car club instead of owning a car will save you around £1,500 a year in costs, including tax, insurance, maintenance and fuel, which are all included in the membership fees and hourly rates.

Car clubs get glowing reports from members. These people can always go back to owning a car, but most wouldn't dream of it, because the car club is so much better.

These schemes work best in cities where there are lots of people within reach of a club parking space, but rural car clubs are beginning to spread out as well.

15 SHOP LOCALLY

In the UK now, about one in ten journeys by car is to go shopping for food, and around 5 per cent of all mileage is used for this purpose.

So, walking to the local shops can make a real difference in reducing congestion and cutting your fuel costs, not forgetting increasing the exercise you get.

If you can't get everything you need nearby at the moment, switching just some of your shopping trips to your local shops – for those couple of items you forgot perhaps – cuts out a car journey every time.

It's not just the environment that gains from local shopping. A wide range of local shops is important in building safe and friendly communities, so supporting your local independent shops helps make the streets safer for others who might be nervous about walking around the local area and therefore tempted to use their car to go further away.

Why not start buying a few regular items from local independent shops and then asking them to stock more of the other things you need? Eventually you might be able to get everything you need nearby and cut out those trips to the supermarket altogether.

TOP-UP SHOP 16

Most people do one main grocery shop per week. Surveys have shown that on average we spend 80 per cent of our family food budgets in just one trip to the supermarket.

Lots of food goes to waste as a result. More than a third of the food we buy ends up in the bin; some as peelings and offcuts, but a lot simply goes off in the fridge, cupboard or vegetable rack, because we buy too much at once or don't plan ahead and end up with ingredients we never use for cooking meals.

Most of us already use other shops in between main shopping trips in order to top up our cupboards with things such as bread and milk that run out or go stale. These top-up visits to the shops tend not to be special trips but instead are done on the way back from work, or in combination with other journeys, so are very efficient and have little impact on the planet.

So, one way to help cut your carbon footprint is to give up the weekly shop and do all your shopping in lots of smaller top-up shops instead, fitting them into your regular routine. By doing this, you can avoid extra travelling to buy your groceries, and can waste less and eat fresher food as well.

17 GET THINGS DELIVERED

Opting for home delivery instead of driving to the supermarket can save plenty of carbon emissions and, if more of us did it, would also do a lot to reduce local congestion.

Of course, delivery vehicles still take to the roads, but they can deliver to several houses in one trip and save on the total number of journeys. Studies across Europe have shown that if each delivery replaces a shopping trip by car, home shopping results in more than a 70 per cent reduction in the traffic miles involved in getting goods to your house.

Only around 10 per cent of people use home shopping for groceries now, so making more use of these services could really transform our streets. In addition, the more people using a delivery service, the more efficient it gets, as this makes it easier to plan delivery rounds and to drop off more items per trip.

These transport benefits make getting local, organic vegetables delivered through a box scheme one of the greenest ever ways to shop, especially if you can find one that delivers by bike.

But don't stop with veg; there are plenty of other items you can buy this way:

• Groceries (try to find a service that uses local shops, or a warehouse system, rather than one that simply picks things up from a supermarket)

• Shoes and clothes (I buy almost all my shoes online now, because it's so much easier than running around lots of different shops)

• Music and films (where you know exactly what you are getting)

LOVE THE BUS AND TRAM

When many people need to move in the same direction, the idea of sharing a large vehicle rather than all travelling in separate cars is pure common sense, whether or not you are worried about climate change.

Providing regular public transport services along main routes goes a long way back in history.

Starting in the 1600s, cross-country stagecoaches became very popular in the days before railways, and their routes became dotted with thriving towns and coaching inns where horses could be changed and passengers refreshed. The first horse-drawn urban omnibuses began in the 1820s, while cable cars and electric trams on rails were introduced in cities from the 1870s.

Unfortunately, the explosion of motor car use in the middle of the last century meant lots of tram systems were dismantled. But, today, where trams have survived or been reintroduced, they are more popular than buses, because they offer a smoother ride and suffer fewer delays.

Towns and cities with good public transport services have lower levels of car ownership. In central London, less than half of households own a car and more than five million people catch the bus every day.

If you don't have services covering the journeys you need to make, there's no point in urging you to use the bus or tram. But, if there is a bus you could use but don't, here are some benefits you might not have thought of, which might encourage you to use it more.

In addition, if you have poor services in your area, here are some ideas on how to campaign to improve them.

18 SAVE CARBON ON THE BUS

A bus has a bigger engine than a car and, as a vehicle, puts out lots of carbon dioxide. However, even with relatively few passengers, the emissions per person are much less than in the car.

An ordinary diesel bus gets around six miles to the gallon in the city and emits around 1,300 grams of carbon dioxide per kilometre. So even with only twenty passengers, this is just 65 grams per person for each kilometre travelled – far less than the average car at 169 grams per kilometre. And in a full double-decker with seventy-five passengers, each person has a tiny emissions total of just 17 grams per kilometre.

Hybrid buses, which combine a diesel engine with an electric motor, are being introduced in lots of cities. These have a lower carbon footprint (around 750 grams of carbon dioxide per kilometre for an average bus), and bring benefits for air quality as well.

Data in grams of carbon dioxide, per kilometre, per passenger

**Hybrid bus
75 passengers:
10g each**

**Double-decker
75 passengers:
17g each**

**Hybrid bus
20 passengers:
38g each**

**Diesel bus
20 passengers:
65g each**

**Average car
1 person:
169g each**

19 MULTI-TASKING ON THE BUS

Regardless of carbon considerations, there are lots of good reasons to be on the bus or tram. Here are five benefits of public transport you might not have considered.

1. You can read a book

On the bus, you can enjoy a good novel, read the newspaper or even catch up on work, unlike in the car where listening to the radio or music system is the only option.

2. You'll be less stressed

Because you can read to take your mind off delays, and always have the option of getting out and walking instead, buses in traffic jams are much less frustrating places to be than stuck in your car. And, of course, the more people who decide to take the bus, the fewer traffic jams there will be anyway.

3. You can use your mobile phone

Using a mobile phone while driving is illegal, because it has been shown to be a dangerous distraction. On the bus, as long as you keep your voice low, answering the phone is not punishable.

4. You can have a drink

Drinking and driving can be deadly, but if you're catching the bus home, having a glass of wine with dinner is not a problem. Cheers!

5. You'll be thinner

Even that short walk to the bus or tram stop contributes to your physical wellbeing and helps to keep the weight off, compared with simply walking down the driveway to your car.

20 GET A BETTER SERVICE

Bus companies are usually profit-seeking enterprises. They don't like to run services that no one will use, since they need our ticket money to keep going.

So, if a bus takes an illogical or out-of-date route, making it unsuitable for people in your area, it can pay to let the bus company know and suggest some changes. Otherwise, faced with fewer passengers, they may cancel it altogether.

Similarly, if you can demonstrate local demand for a new route, the company may be very interested to hear about a new way for them to make money.

If there's an obvious gap in your local services, why not get a petition together? Place it in local libraries, collect signatures along the route – perhaps at a school, leisure centre or shopping parade – then present your case to the company and your local council to show them how much good the new route will do.

GREENER CARS

The issue that first got me involved with green campaigning was the growing number of big 4x4 vehicles being used instead of ordinary cars in London. With several schools just up the hill from my house, I was waiting for the bus every morning and watching a queue of heavy off-roaders going past that were being used just to take one parent and one child a mile or two down the road.

The fashion for big, tall cars, has influenced the rest of us in our vehicle choices, too. Despite advances in technology, the average efficiency of a car on our streets has hardly improved in the last few years and we are way behind the targets we set in the 1990s. This is partly the fault of car companies trying to sell us bigger cars that bring them bigger profits. However, in the end, our choice of vehicle is down to us.

I got a bit carried away and set up a whole campaign to deal with the problem of 4x4s, but you don't have to go that far. With air quality failing to improve in our towns and cities, and with danger to pedestrians very closely linked to the weight and height of cars, making a personal choice to drive a smaller, more efficient vehicle is one of the best things you can do to help improve our local environment and cut down on your carbon emissions.

There are, of course, lots of other ways to travel, and this book has many ideas for avoiding car journeys. However, if you do have to use a car for some trips, here are some ways to cut down on the damage caused – and save you money in fuel costs, too.

21 GET THE BEST CAR

Start by finding the greenest car you can for the type of vehicle you want. The range of fuel efficiencies between very similar cars is vast – even if you need a big 4x4, you can find well-designed cars that are more than twice as efficient as the worst models.

Do some simple research before setting out for the showroom by looking up the best cars on the internet. There are several sites that give the fuel efficiency (in grams of carbon dioxide per kilometre) for all the cars on the market. Most sites let you choose the type of vehicle and the type of fuel before giving you a list of the best cars in that class.

And remember, it's not all about fancy new technology. If you just need a car to get you from A to B, there are plenty of well-made small models that use petrol or diesel, but are just as fuel efficient as the hybrids.

Don't forget safety. For cars on sale in Europe, you can check the crash-test scores for passenger safety, the safety of children in the back and for pedestrians at the Euro NCAP crash-testing site.

See the back of this book for more information and links.

CONSIDER A HYBRID CAR 22

Hybrid cars are gaining in popularity, even though they cost 10–20 per cent more than a petrol or diesel equivalent. The technology they use is really clever, combining a petrol engine with an electric motor that is charged up using energy recovered by the brakes. The choice of engine used at each point on the journey is controlled by an on-board computer, which also shows exactly where the energy is flowing with a nifty dashboard display.

Hybrid cars are almost exactly like a normal automatic car to drive, and never need to be plugged in, because all the energy they use comes from petrol. They are a lower carbon option because they make much better use of the petrol than a normal car, where the energy from braking is simply lost in heat through the brake pads.

There are only a handful of hybrids on the market at the moment, but more are in the pipeline and the prices should start to come down soon. You can even catch hybrid buses in many cities; London now has a range of single- and double-deckers on the road.

23 GREENER DRIVING SKILLS

The fuel-efficiency figures given in the official statistics aren't often what people achieve when driving in the real world, because they are measured under strict test conditions.

However, you can get the most out of your car (and get much closer to these figures) by adopting some simple techniques for greener driving.

1. Set off straightaway

Leaving your car running for ages to warm up doesn't just annoy your neighbours, it is also a complete waste of fuel.

2. Switch off in long queues

Opinions differ on the exact numbers, but restarting the engine uses less fuel than somewhere between 10 and 20 seconds of idling. So, in a long traffic queue, turning off the engine is good practice. Stay alert so you can switch it back on quickly when the traffic moves again. A hybrid engine will do this automatically, which is part of the reason it's so efficient.

3. Keep the speed down on the motorway

The optimum driving speed for good fuel efficiency is about 55mph (90kph). Above this, fuel use goes up around 15 per cent for every extra 10mph. In the UK, driving at 85mph on the motorway is illegal, but many people do it anyway, without realising they are using up to 25 per cent more fuel than they would by sticking to the 70mph speed limit.

4. Don't carry things you don't need

Heavy items left in the boot and unused roof racks all reduce your fuel efficiency.

5. Drive smoothly

Don't accelerate up to a red light and avoid too much braking. Think ahead and try to drive at a smooth, even pace for maximum fuel efficiency and less wear and tear.

6. Watch your rpm

Your car's engine is working at its most efficient when it is turning at between 1,500 and 2,500 revolutions per minute. The display on the dashboard will show the rpm, and this can climb up to 4,000 or more if you are in the wrong gear. Change up a gear smoothly when the rpm count reaches around 2,500 for petrol cars and 2,000 for diesel cars and you'll notice a real difference in fuel efficiency.

24 ELECTRIC CITY CARS

Electric cars are ideal for the city. They use no fossil fuels directly and have no exhaust pipe, so are great for improving air quality. They are also really quiet, and because they are generally fairly small, contribute less to congestion. They are a fantastic alternative for shorter journeys that are too long for a bike.

Electric city cars need to be charged up between uses, usually via a normal plug socket. They will do between thirty and two hundred miles per charge, depending on the terrain and the model, but don't have maximum speeds as high as a petrol car, so are best suited to stop-start traffic in cities.

In the UK, the most widely available electric car is called the G-Wiz. It has four seats (although the back seats only really fit children), a range of around 40 miles and a maximum speed of 40 mph. In London, they can park in the centre of town for nothing and pay no congestion charges, so you can often see them making their way quietly through the rush hour.

25 WHY NOT A MOTORBIKE?

If your regular journeys can't be shared with others, and are not easy to walk, cycle or take with public transport, a motorbike or scooter could be a good investment.

Compared with a car, a motorbike takes up much less space, is easier to park and has a much lower carbon footprint.

For city use, motor scooters are the greenest choice, as they generally have smaller engines. You don't need special clothing to ride one, and can even wear a skirt if you like.

As with cars, the fuel efficiency of motorcycles will vary, so check the figures when choosing a model, and look out for the electric motorbikes that are just starting to be produced.

Finally, make sure you have the right licence and get training on how to ride safely. Motorcycle accidents are, sadly, more common than for other forms of transport, but by getting a good trainer and following their advice, you can keep yourself out of trouble.

SCHOOL TRAVEL

A quarter of journeys taken by children under 16 are to school and back. These trips are where we learn travelling habits and skills that we'll keep for life, whether it's riding a bike on the road confidently, learning to cross the road safely, becoming familiar with bus routes or – less positively – getting into the bad habit of a sedentary lifestyle that relies on the car.

If we help build greener habits in children, we gain long-term benefits for society and the planet, but we also see immediate benefits, too, from improving local air quality to making our streets friendlier and safer from crime and traffic danger.

The trip to school is an excellent place to start making greener travel choices, since school travel is becoming less sustainable with every year that passes.

Around one in twenty of all car trips are now made to and from school, and at 8.50 in the morning in urban areas, one in five cars is taking a child to school, so the school run also plays its part in creating carbon emissions and congestion in the rush hour.

With the majority of primary schools within one and half miles of home, and most secondary schools within walking or cycling distance, or well-served by public transport, there are many ways to make a real difference by greening the school run.

26 WALK TO SCHOOL

As a child, I was allowed to walk to and from primary school with a friend who lived next door from the age of seven, and this really helped to make me more independent and confident. Hardly anyone at my school travelled by car, so I was shocked when I found out that now only around half of primary school children walk and that around 40 per cent are being taken to school in the car.

There is no good reason for this decline in children walking to school. The risk from strangers is much lower than we think and keeping children in 'captivity' indoors and in the car is very irrational when there are now many safeguards.

In fact, the risks from becoming obese and inactive are far higher, as is the danger of increasing traffic. A child is in fifty times more danger of being killed in a car accident (as a pedestrian or a passenger) than they are of being killed by a stranger, and a study in the UK showed that children walking to school used up more calories doing this in a week than they used up in formal PE lessons.

Start creating confident, streetwise kids by walking with them to school while they are small. Make the journey fun and use it as an opportunity to get to know your area and observe the world around you. Play games, such as spotting different kinds of trees and plants, or number games with car registration plates.

Deciding when to walk on their own should be up to the children themselves. Let them tell you when they are confident, and start by arranging for them to walk with friends from nearby.

After walking with you for years, they should be well equipped to look after themselves, but make sure they know these tips, too:

• Know your route and stick to it
• Know how to cross the road safely and never take risks with traffic
• Stay with the friends you are walking with, even if you have an argument
• Say no to strangers, no matter how nice they seem
• Know places of safety along the route, such as shops, libraries or the police station
• Be visible – wear bright colours and high-visibility accessories, such as wristbands or stickers on bags

27 SET UP A WALKING BUS

With an increasing number of children being driven to school, many areas suffer from dangerous congestion in the mornings, which has prompted parents and schools to come up with a brilliant solution: the walking bus, or crocodile.

A walking bus involves two or three parents each day supervising up to twenty children, who walk in one group along a fixed route to school, picking up other children on the way. The children all wear bright waistcoats and the 'bus conductors' may use a trolley to help carry school bags, making the whole thing an easy, fun way to share the job of getting kids to school and keeping them active.

Setting up a walking bus is relatively simple, especially if parents walking with their children already meet up on the route and know each other. A walking bus shares responsibility and gives parents free time when it's not their turn to supervise, so there are lots of good reasons to make the effort to push the idea forward.

Talk to the school and your local council's school travel advisers, who can help with things such as police checks, advertising the bus to other parents and drawing up rotas. You could even get sponsorship from local businesses to help buy high-visibility clothing – it's a great advert for them, and the walking bus as a whole is a great advert for walking to school.

28 BIKE TO SCHOOL

Kids need exercise. An hour a day is recommended by experts, and cycling to school is an excellent way to build this into their daily lives, rather than making it a special activity needing lots of organisation.

In Denmark, 60 per cent of children cycle to school. It's part of the culture there, thanks to excellent cycle routes and a real commitment from schools to support cycling. In the UK, things are rather different, with just 1 per cent of primary school children and 3 per cent of secondary children getting on their bikes.

With training and a helmet, any risks from cycling are outweighed by the benefits of being healthy, active and independent, and cycling in the early years also helps children to grow up into healthier adults. After all, riding a bike is like, well, riding a bike! You never forget how to do it once you learn and it's a valuable life skill.

Parents can do a lot to encourage children to cycle, from providing a bike in the first place, to helping children to master the basic skills. Schools can do a lot, too, providing training and a secure place to keep bikes during the school day, and making sure children don't have to carry lots of heavy books.

29 AFTER-SCHOOL TRAVEL

At the moment, children make over half their journeys as passengers in cars. So, as a parent, you can promote their health and reduce your family's carbon footprint by changing the way you travel outside school hours.

If you're going to a football match or to the swimming pool, why not take your children on the bus, or walk with them if it's less than a couple of miles away? Without the stress of concentrating on driving, these journeys can give you time to have real, focused conversations with your children, to get to know your area better, and helps give them the confidence to use these modes of travel on their own when they grow older.

Cycling with your children is healthy for everyone, and is a great way to teach your children road skills before you let them cycle on their own.

SCHOOL TRIPS 30

If you are a teacher, or a parent who helps organise days out for children at school, why not think about ways of making these more active?

Kids are full of energy, and on a school trip tend to get very excitable. As a result, keeping them quiet in a museum or stately home can be very difficult. Choose trips that involve more activity to help the children let off steam, and improve their health and fitness as well.

See if you can find active local activities, such as a guided walk around a forest or sculpture park, a trip to an adventure playground or assault course, or a day filled with outdoor activities, such as archery or abseiling. Look out for the increasing number of environmental groups providing green activities especially for schools, such as pond cleaning, tree planting or stone-wall building.

WORK TRAVEL

Travel to work is a major part of our day-to-day mileage, accounting for about a fifth of the distance we travel and an even larger amount of the time we spend travelling, because so much of it is done at busy times. After all, without work travel there would be no rush hour!

The length of the average trip to work has gone up 6 per cent in the last ten years, but the time spent on the journey has increased by 15 per cent. On average now, working people spend an hour each weekday just commuting.

Many of our longer trips are made for business, too. Company cars travel twice as far as private cars – nearly 20,000 miles a year on average.

There are benefits to both businesses and their workers for making work travel more sustainable. Congestion and delays cost money and can create problems with recruitment, if potential staff think the journey is too difficult. And don't forget that reducing carbon dioxide emissions and creating a greener workplace is also very good for your organisation's image.

There is plenty of scope to reduce the number of cars on the road by sharing lifts to work. Making it easier for employees to get to work by public transport, cycling and walking helps them to be more active and makes them healthier, less stressed and more motivated. Employers can also help the environment and improve productivity by helping people to work at home more often.

Some of the tips in this section are things you can do as an employee on your own. Others are things your workplace needs to help with, but you can play an important part in getting these initiatives off the ground. If you're the boss, you can make an even greater difference – all these ideas will work best if managers get involved and really want to help.

31 | **WORK FROM HOME**

Less than one in twenty people works at home regularly, but almost one in five of us could work at least some of the time away from the office.

For the planet, the main benefits of home-working come through avoiding the carbon dioxide emissions involved in the trip to work. Since slow, congested traffic creates higher carbon emissions per mile, the savings from people spending just one day at home every fortnight could cut rush hour traffic by 10 per cent and carbon emissions by even more if everyone's journey speeds up.

There are other benefits to staying at home to work some of the time. Away from the chattering of colleagues, it can be easier to work on a project that needs a lot of concentrated attention. Staying at home can be better for work-life balance too; you can spend your lunch hour catching up on housework and be at home when the kids get back from school.

In winter, carbon savings are less, however, because heating one workplace for hundreds of people is less energy-intensive than heating everyone's house individually. When you are working at home, try to minimise this effect by heating just the room you are working in, rather than the whole house.

32 TRY CAR SHARING

Commuters in cars are much more likely to be travelling alone compared with the average driver. In the USA, nine out of ten commuters travel to work by car and the vast majority travel alone, and in the UK, more than 80 per cent of people who drive to work don't share the car with anyone else.

The workplace is ideal for organising car sharing. With everyone coming to the same building every day (and because everyone is known to the organisation), there is a ready-made pool of trustworthy lift-sharers who can be put in touch with one another.

To help people find compatible partners for lift-sharing, a good idea is to organise 'postcode coffee meetings', where people from the same area can meet up and find people to share the driving with.

Anyone could organise this initiative, but employers can make a big impact on the success of these schemes by providing incentives (such as reserved parking spaces) for car-sharers and by guaranteeing people a ride home by taxi if a crisis means their lift lets them down.

In practice, these guarantees are hardly ever used, but having them in place really helps to reassure people that they won't get stranded.

MAKE TRAVEL PLANS 33

A long-term plan to make workplace travel greener can make all the difference. Everyone benefits if a business helps its employees to travel to work in greener and more efficient ways – from people living in the surrounding area, who will enjoy less congestion and fewer cars parking on local streets, to the workers themselves, who will spend less time sitting in traffic and arrive at work happier and less stressed.

There is plenty of detailed advice available from sustainable travel organisations to help a company set up and implement a green travel plan, and more information is included at the back of this book.

The key thing is to start by getting information on where you are now – find out where employees live, how they are getting to work, and what problems are stopping them travelling by greener methods. Then set some realistic targets and bring in a range of measures to achieve them.

What you choose to do will depend on your workplace. For example, if you have most people living within three miles, encouraging cycling will be more important than if the majority of employees live in a town six miles away.

34 WHAT THE BOSS CAN DO

If you are an employee, there's plenty you can do to convince your bosses that encouraging greener travel to work will pay off. But both individual measures and full-scale travel plans work much better when senior management is involved.

If you're the boss, you're in a great place to get things started. You are likely to need a range of 'carrots and sticks' – real incentives to take the car less often, combined with real action to make greener choices more attractive.

It could be as simple as putting in bike parking and a shower, or getting the council to move the bus stop nearer to your offices if it's just that little bit too far away. Remember to keep everyone on side, by bringing in 'sticks', such as reducing the number of car parking spaces, after you've provided 'carrots', such as parking spaces for car-sharers.

Once you're making progress, tell people about your success and build up momentum for more ambitious plans. For business travel, companies can make a lot of savings – in carbon and in cash – by using car-share companies to provide pool cars, rather than giving out individual company cars. By also offering company bikes, travelcards and other benefits, your employees can simply and painlessly make greener travel choices on the company's behalf.

35 BUSINESS TRIPS BY TRAIN

In contrast to driving along the motorway and the bargain, no-frills experience offered by cheap flights, business travel by train is a joy.

Even in standard class on a train, you get a seat at least as comfortable as a business class seat on a plane. And, unlike on the plane or in the car, you can also stay in telephone contact with the office and use a decent size table. You can even get wireless internet access on modern locomotives.

I travel by train all over the country for my work, and always use the journey to read reports, write documents and catch up with the office in comfort. Even if I wasn't an environmentalist, there's no contest for me when compared with business trips by car or plane. It's even quicker in a lot of cases, since you travel at high speed from city centre to city centre and don't have to worry about getting into town from the airport when you land.

Unfortunately, company expense systems can create perverse disincentives to rail travel. A simple mileage allowance for business travel can mean late-booked train tickets aren't fully covered, and can encourage people to use their cars and pocket the change if the allowance covers more than the cost of petrol. Make sure your company promotes rail travel for business trips by paying full expenses rather than a mileage allowance.

36 MEET BY VIDEO OR PHONE

Working trips add a lot to our carbon footprints, with around a fifth of long-distance travel miles being used for business reasons.

Cutting down on business travel makes a lot of sense, since no matter how comfortable your train seat, travel time is never as effective as being at your desk. There are lots of new (and relatively old) technologies that can help to reduce the time, money and carbon spent on business travel.

Plenty of business meetings don't need to have all the participants around the same table. In the Green Party, our Executive members are based all over the country, and if an important issue comes up between meetings, we often have a phone conference. There's a certain degree of etiquette you need to learn for one of these (mainly not to interrupt people!), but they can be an excellent way to focus on one issue and make quick decisions.

For events such as conferences and presentations, seeing the person you are talking to can be more important, and video conferences are an ideal low-carbon way of achieving this. A video link can also be a handy way to get an important speaker, who can't make it in person, to address your event.

Early video-conferencing equipment was huge, clunky and very expensive. But now, with better communications networks, there are more affordable options, including simple webcams for one-to-one meetings, which use free software and cost little to set up.

Data in grams of carbon dioxide, per kilometre, per passenger

Full coach:
9g each

Average car
(four people):
42g each

Electric train:
51g each

Diesel train:
69g each

Average car
(one person):
169g each

Plane
(average occupancy):
230–510g each

LONG-DISTANCE TRAVEL

For longer trips, walking and cycling aren't an option, making travelling in greener ways mainly a case of minimising carbon emissions rather than cutting them out altogether.

For most people, the choice of how to travel depends on speed, convenience and cost. Despite the fact that fuel makes up a large part of the resources used for travelling, cost is often not a good indicator of carbon emissions. Aircraft fuel is completely untaxed, so airlines are, in fact, receiving a bigger subsidy than even the best funded rail system.

As a result, an increasing number of long trips in Europe and America are being taken by plane, despite the fact that, for trips of less than 500 miles, the train is usually quicker and more convenient.

Even in the UK, where hardly any journeys are more than 500 miles long on our small island, 39 per cent of journeys over 350 miles are now taken by aeroplane. The most common mode of travel is the car, at 42 per cent, with just 12 per cent of people travelling by train and 5 per cent by coach.

Luckily, there is lots of scope for increasing our use of more environmentally friendly modes of transport for long distances and we can also reduce the impact of car journeys by filling up vehicles more efficiently.

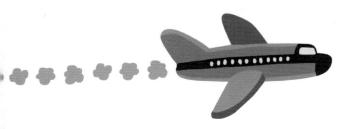

37 TAKE YOUR TIME

Most long-distance journeys are taken for personal and leisure reasons, so it is relatively easy to switch these to more enjoyable and, importantly, lower carbon ways of travelling. Being more relaxed about your schedule opens up lots of different options and means you can more easily use different modes of transport for different stages of the journey.

If you are going on a long trip, why not break up a car journey into stages by stopping off to visit friends, or stay overnight at a hotel and see some extra attractions, rather than flying overhead without taking notice of the places in between home and your eventual destination?

Travelling overland provides the ideal opportunity to hop between cities on your route and spend a day in each one. This is a much better way to explore than flying out to each city for multiple weekend breaks.

38 STRESS LESS ON THE TRAIN

The number of people taking planes or driving for long distances is a bit of a mystery to me. I hate being on a plane and really dislike having to drive on the motorway. In my experience, both are really stressful, uncomfortable ways of getting about.

In contrast, I love being on the train. The journey is smooth, generally very fast and predictable, you have a table to work on and you can while away the time in comfort playing cards or having a picnic.

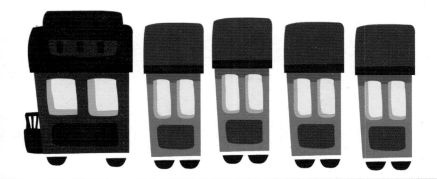

The view from a train is also one of the most relaxing sights in the world, with the countryside sweeping by, unbroken by ugly signs, lorries and other motorway accessories. You can also get up, stretch your legs and walk to the buffet for a change of scenery.

All in all, taking the train means your holiday starts as soon as you leave the house.

And then there are the green credentials of taking the train. While not as low in carbon emissions as the coach, the train beats a solo car trip by miles at around 51 grams per kilometre per passenger for an electric train and 69 grams per kilometre for an older diesel train.

39 COACHES

Coach travel is a sadly neglected form of low-carbon, long-distance transport. This is a real shame, because coaches can be much more flexible than trains. They don't needs lots of permanent infrastructure and, with a full complement of passengers, provide the lowest carbon form of powered transport around.

Even at average occupancy, long-distance express coaches emit just 29 grams of carbon per passenger kilometre and a full coach emits just 9 grams per kilometre per person.

When planning a journey that can't be done by train, or if the train is very expensive, don't forget to check out the coach service before deciding to drive all the way to your destination. Although coaches aren't always as quick or as comfortable as trains, this is changing and they do have lots of the other benefits, such as the chance to read and relax rather than focus on the road ahead. Coaches are also very affordable compared with train travel, and with so-called cheap flights.

In Spain, coach travel is the norm for long-distance journeys. This is because they have an excellent system of convenient, comfortable services, which means that people there take the coach twice as often as they take the train. There's no reason why, with more people needing to travel in greener ways, coach travel everywhere couldn't be this good.

Things are improving in the UK, too. I often get on a double-decker coach from Oxford to London, which has extra leg room, very comfortable seats (some with tables) and even power points for laptops and mobile phones. If you haven't taken the coach for a while, check out the new services and you might get a surprise.

40 SHARE THE JOURNEY

For long distances, sharing lifts makes even more sense than it does for shorter journeys. Sharing the cost of fuel with several others can make a car journey the cheapest way to travel, and also a surprisingly low-carbon one as well.

In an average car, filling it up with four people reduces the carbon emissions to just 42 grams per kilometre, which makes it less carbon-heavy than a train, although nowhere near as efficient as a coach.

There are other benefits to sharing a car on a long journey. Taking turns with driving reduces the need to rest along the way, and having interesting travelling companions can help to take some of the boredom out of a long spell on the motorway.

For personal journeys over longer distances, lift-sharing websites can be really useful for putting groups of car-sharers in touch. This can work even better than for short trips to work, since everyone just needs to be from the same town to make it worthwhile, rather than from the same neighbourhood.

See the information section at the end of this book for websites that help you to organise shared journeys by car.

GREENER HOLIDAYS

Sometimes I think adverts have made us forget what holidays are for. We've all been sold the same image of the 'ideal holiday': a palm tree and a stretch of white sand next to a turquoise sea. But is that really what makes for the perfect break? Does going far away guarantee having a better time? And does a few days of tropical weather make spending twelve hours on a plane worth the hassle?

Over three quarters of parents say that spending quality time with the kids is the main thing they want from a holiday. Yet eight out of ten families have a stressful time on their annual break, with bored children proving the main problem. Surveys show that action and adventure are what kids really want, and that even grown-ups want more from a holiday than a couple of weeks on a sun lounger.

Interesting activities, great food and comfortable accommodation don't require getting on a plane. In fact, most of us can find perfect holiday destinations much closer to home. And, despite the excitement of take-off, travelling further afield by train can be much more rewarding than flying.

Here are some greener ways to have a great holiday while leaving out the airport.

41 | STAY CLOSER TO HOME

It's hard to think of a less relaxing way to start a break than spending hours in an airport and then squashed onto a long flight, so I avoid it whenever possible.

Luckily, the UK has everything I need for the vast majority of my holidays, from the most fantastic range of beaches anywhere in the world, to hills and mountains that are just the right height to walk up without needing rock-climbing gear.

The UK is also packed with history, with more world heritage sites on our islands than in the whole of the USA, including Stonehenge, the Dorset and East Devon Jurassic Coast, castles in North Wales and the city of Bath.

The perfect holiday will be different for different people, but you might be surprised at what you enjoy once you try it. I persuaded members of my family to join me in a cottage in Cumbria last year and we had a great time wandering over hills, mountains and by lakes, as well as eating and drinking in local pubs. Although they had never been on a walking holiday before, they all had such a great time that they immediately booked the same cottage for another visit this year.

If you're not from the UK, don't let me persuade you this is the only place to visit. Your own country will have its own attractions, its own beautiful geography, its own history and plenty of great holiday destinations, so don't neglect these!

42 ROMANCE OF A TRAIN HOLIDAY

When you take a holiday by train, you really know you're
travelling. Watching the landscape change as you move from
country to country, tunnelling under mountains and whizzing
across bridges, you get the very best view of the world passing
by and really appreciate the distance you have covered when you
reach your destination.

Rightly, some of the most famous romantic journeys are by train,
and well-known trains outnumber famous planes by the dozen.
But you don't have to travel on the Orient Express or the Trans-
Siberian Railway to make the most of the romance of holidaying
by train.

Long-distance, inter-city trains with sleeper cars and restaurants
can get you almost anywhere, and good travel agents can book
your trains as well as your hotels for a holiday that really lets you
see the world. Yes, it takes longer to get there, but on the train
your holiday starts as soon as you leave home.

See the links at the back of this book for more on booking
international train journeys in Europe and beyond.

43 GOING BY SHIP

Sea travel doesn't lack romance either. Unfortunately, large cruise ships can be as carbon-intensive as aeroplanes per passenger kilometre (although, since you also live on board, the carbon cost includes emissions from accommodation and food, which you'd have to add to the emissions from your flight to get the total for a flying holiday).

For shorter journeys to simply get you across the water, travelling by ferry saves carbon compared with the plane. The carbon emissions vary according to exactly what type of ship you take. A super-fast ferry or catamaran can be as carbon-heavy as flying, but ferry travel is generally better, ranging from 50–200 grams per kilometre per passenger.

44 CAR HOLIDAYS

A holiday by car can be a good choice if the train is very expensive or doesn't go to your destination. Four people with luggage in the average car will create around the same amount of carbon dioxide per person as if you took the train, so this is a very good choice for a family holiday.

Travelling by car gives you more options when you reach your destination. Although I wouldn't recommend going by car to a big city, camping trips and adventure holidays can be enhanced by having your own transport to help you explore.

In Europe, a good way of taking your car but saving on driving is to use the various Motorail services. These let you put your car on a train so you can relax on the way and then drive off at the end of the journey. You can cross the channel with the Eurotunnel service, and use Motorail to get around most of France and Germany in the summer, and even use it to travel to Italy, Greece, Croatia and Turkey.

With a family of four, the car beats the plane every time. However, if you are travelling on your own over a long distance and have a car with a big engine, your emissions can come close to those of a flight. Short-haul flights are much higher in emissions per kilometre, thanks to the high energy needed for take-off and landing. So, as a general rule, for solo journeys opt for the car for anything under 1,000 km, then think about the plane.

TRAVEL BETTER WHEN YOU FLY

The facts on flying and climate change are the subject of much debate and can be confusing. Currently, flying makes up only a few per cent of the UK's emissions. However, within a few decades, air travel could be producing more carbon dioxide than our country's entire target if planned expansion goes ahead.

The easiest way to see the impact of flying on your personal emissions is with a website-based carbon calculator. Adding just one long-haul flight to the sums can double your carbon total.

My favourite way of dealing with climate change is for all of us to have a carbon allowance that we have to live within. Under this system, it's the total amount of carbon dioxide we create that matters, not where it comes from. So, if we wanted to save up our allowance for a long trip somewhere exotic, we could, but we'd have to make a lot of savings elsewhere to cover it.

While this system is still only a good idea in the minds of some campaigners and politicians (although it is gaining support all the time), we can use the same principle in the meantime to make sure we cut all our carbon, not just our flights, and keep flying in perspective as one part of a bigger problem.

The solution is not simply never to fly again, but to cut carbon right across our lifestyles, and to think carefully before flying, reducing the number of flights we take to an absolute minimum to keep our overall carbon footprint low.

Here are some tips that will help you to get more out of your air miles by travelling less often and staying for longer (rather than taking lots of mini-breaks), leaving behind real benefits in the places we visit, doing green work while we're there and supporting greener businesses and community projects.

These actions will give us a much cleaner conscience than if we fly off every five minutes and offset.

45 TO OFFSET OR NOT?

Carbon offsetting is one of those things that seemed like a good idea at the time, but which has proved almost completely impossible to do effectively.

There are three major problems with the concept of flying now and then paying for someone else to offset your emissions later:

1. The savings might not happen or take too long

When you fly, the emissions are put right into the atmosphere straightaway, while offsetting projects that plant trees count the carbon the trees will capture during their whole lifetime (perhaps one hundred years). The problem with this is that there's no guarantee all the trees planted will survive that long, and the carbon you emitted is left hanging around doing damage in the meantime.

Offsetting companies have also got into difficulties with schemes that make savings through development projects in poor countries. Many of these projects take ages to get going or collapse before they are completed, meaning your offset might not happen at all.

2. The savings could have happened anyway

It's very hard to be sure that a project paid for by offsetting would not have found some other way to get going. Again, tree-planting schemes have had problems here, with offsetting companies buying up rights to plantations that were going ahead anyway.

Many charities are already providing solar panels, low-energy stoves and light bulbs to developing countries without needing to take money from frequent flyers, which is why offsetting schemes sometimes struggle to prove their savings are really new reductions to count against your flight.

3. Measuring savings is almost impossible

Working out the amount of carbon taken up by trees, or avoided by providing solar panels, is really difficult. Eco-systems and economies are very complex, and there are always a range of effects created by these projects. For example, changing land use may mean some carbon dioxide is released from the soil as well as taken up by trees, or the availability of cheap electricity may mean people use more of other resources, too.

Because of these difficulties, the Gold Standard scheme, set up by green organisations in Europe to certify offsets, has approved

only a handful of schemes due to the difficulties of measuring the effects of each project.

Now, don't get me wrong. It is good to donate to environmental projects and a very good time to do it is when you are booking a flight. However, to think of the money you donate as actually cancelling out the carbon from your flight is a mistake, and not a good reason to fly more than you have to.

46 GO FOR LONGER

I really support the maxim that travel broadens the mind, but I don't think we need to see the world one weekend at a time and rack up a huge carbon footprint in the process. Making the most of the carbon we emit while flying can be as simple as travelling less often and for longer.

I have, in the past, taken almost every kind of holiday, from a weekend city break to a fortnight in the Mediterranean and a far-flung gap-year trip for several months. Of all of these, the one that I still remember the most is that one long trip. While the others fade away, I can still vividly remember the people I met, the things I saw and the places I lived in, and I think I always will.

It's important that we all take time out like this sometimes – not just after leaving school, but at other times in our lives. A year spent travelling around the world between jobs gives new perspectives that you can bring to the rest of your career, and a well-earned few months off after retiring can be the ideal way to adjust to your new status.

A longer trip, planned well ahead, also allows you to do your homework, learn a little of the local language and really get to know the places you visit while you are there. This is much better than relying on tour-operator excursions and day trips to pick up a few bare facts.

If we all followed a different pattern of flying – travelling long-haul very infrequently, but staying for several months each time – we'd benefit more from the experience and, with other savings across the rest of our lifestyles, could still do this within our overall carbon budget.

47 BUY LOCAL STUFF

One way to improve the harm-to-benefit ratio of your holiday is to make sure the economy of the place you visit is improved by your trip.

We all want to bring home souvenirs that remind us of the great times we had, but in lots of places the most obvious souvenir choices aren't locally made goods but T-shirts and plastic models of landmarks which are usually made in China. Buying these does little to bring benefits to the local area (unless, I suppose, you are actually visiting China!).

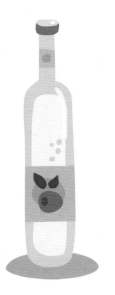

By doing your homework, you'll have found out what the local area is famous for producing, so seek out where these items are being made to make sure the profits go back into the local economy, rather than being whisked away by international companies.

Whether it's honey, wine, lavender, leather goods, ceramics, bamboo, spices, ceramics, books, shoes or fishing tackle, you'll help the local area and end up with a souvenir that is an authentic reminder of your holiday destination.

48 USE LOCAL SERVICES

It's also important that the services you use while on holiday bring benefits to the place you visit. From staying in a hotel to eating out and visiting a museum, providing jobs for local people is the main reason places promote themselves as tourist destinations and try to bring in visitors.

Unfortunately, too many holidays are run by big operators that provide only low-paid, unskilled jobs in big resorts and then take the majority of the profits straight out of the country.

More ethical tourism involves staying in locally owned and run hotels and guesthouses, where people are better paid, have decent working conditions and where all the profits stay within the local area.

Community enterprises can range from small guesthouses in Europe to tropical homestays, where you are housed as guests in a village. In Europe, the USA and other rich countries, small, locally owned hotels and guesthouses can easily be found through conventional travel agencies or on the internet. However, in the developing world, these businesses may not be able to afford to advertise or run a website. Luckily, our desire for more responsible tourism means that agencies to help you find accommodation with real local benefits are now appearing, and you'll find some websites to look at in the information section at the end of this book.

And don't forget to use other local services while you are there – I find that one of the best ways to really get to know a place is to use the local bus!

49 DO GOOD ON HOLIDAY

If you want to travel with a cleaner conscience, have useful skills or want to learn a new one, doing voluntary work abroad is a great way to see a new country and make up (at least partly) for the carbon emissions involved in getting there.

Volunteering organisations, such as the International Voluntary Service, specialise in placing volunteers in a wide range of projects around the world – from caring for children in Europe, to working in a community theatre in India, to cleaning up beaches in Africa. See the links at the end of this book for lots of different ways to volunteer abroad.

For a longer-term placement, why not apply to Voluntary Service Overseas (VSO)? They employ skilled professionals, from engineers to social workers, to spend up to two years using and passing on their skills in countries that need them.

And, of course, you don't have to travel halfway across the world to get involved in conservation work and have an active, green break. In the UK, there are hundreds of opportunities to do green work on holidays with the British Trust for Conservation Volunteers or with local Wildlife Trusts.

50 FIND AN ECO-HOTEL

While there's no point travelling across the world just to stay in a hotel with a low carbon footprint, finding an eco-friendly hotel in a place you are visiting is something every good green wants to do.

There are various ways of tracking down planet-friendly places to stay. Organisations such as Conservation International and online travel agents, such as Responsible Travel, are experts at finding hotels, lodges and apartments that minimise their impact through energy conservation, the efficient use of water, waste minimisation and cooking with local organic produce.

Interestingly, eco-hotels are often found on islands, where the cost of shipping in supplies means that saving energy, using water efficiently, cutting down on waste and pollution, and being more self-sufficient make good business sense as well.

FURTHER INFORMATION

WALKING BACK TO HAPPINESS

Living Streets campaigns to create better streets in towns and cities to help people get around on foot.
www.livingstreets.org.uk

The Ramblers' Association has a wealth of information and advice for walkers at all levels, and can help you find guided walks and signed routes in your area.
www.ramblers.org.uk

In London and other cities, getting about on foot is far more interesting than taking the underground and missing all the sights. Find directions, routes and maps for London, Birmingham, Edinburgh and Newcastle at the Walkit website.
www.walkit.com

The Enjoy England website has a search engine that helps you find attractions and events in your local area, including many guided walks.
www.enjoyengland.com

The Ordnance Survey website has a search function that will find you short walks in any area of the country, posted by users of the site. There are literally thousands to choose from, many less than two miles long, and all with excellent maps, of course.
www.ordnancesurvey.co.uk/oswebsite/leisure/

Walking the Way to Health is an organisation offering guided short walks all over the country for complete beginners and those who want to begin walking for health reasons.
www.whi.org.uk

Longer walks in England are comprehensively covered on the Walking Englishman website.
www.walkingenglishman.com

The best guide to Highland walks in Scotland.
www.walkhighlands.co.uk

The Ramblers' Association in Wales is developing a directory of walks in Wales, all graded for difficulty with accompanying sketch maps.
www.welshwalks.info

THE FREEDOM OF TWO WHEELS

Sustrans is helping to create a national network of cycle routes in the UK and helps promote safer streets and active travel.
www.sustrans.org.uk

The Cyclists' Touring Club is the UK's largest national cycling organisation, founded in 1878 and still helping cyclists and promoting better cycle routes today.
www.ctc.org.uk

Life Cycle UK offers cycle training and information for adults and children starting out on cycling, with a wealth of information for employers wanting to help people cycle to work.
www.lifecycleuk.org.uk

CUTTING DOWN ON CAR JOURNEYS

Find people to share your journeys on the Liftshare website.
www.liftshare.org

'Is Anyone Going To' is another great site for finding car shares.
www.isanyonegoingto.com

Carplus is a national UK charity promoting responsible car use, with a useful map of car clubs across the country.
www.carplus.org.uk

Car clubs in London are listed on this website:
www.londoncarclubs.net

Or find the car clubs covering your area by these companies:
City Car Club
www.citycarclub.co.uk

Streetcar
www.streetcar.co.uk

WhizzGo
www.whizzgo.co.uk

Zipcar
www.zipcar.co.uk

LOVE THE BUS AND TRAM

Traveline is where you can look up local bus timetables anywhere in the UK. I tested it out by getting it to find the one bus from my childhood home into town – it worked a treat.
www.traveline.org.uk

In London, don't simply hop on the Tube. Find out your other options, including trams, riverboats and thousands of buses, using Transport for London's journey planner. It will even find you a suitable route to take by bike or on foot.
www.tfl.gov.uk

Friends of the Earth is a campaigning organisation with active local groups around the country. They can help and support your ideas for better bus services in your area.
www.foe.org.uk

Whether you are saving a bus route or campaigning for a new tram, the Campaign for Better Transport also has advice and information for local transport campaigners.
www.bettertransport.org.uk

GREENER CARS

The Environmental Transport Association has a green car-buyers' guide which is easy to use to find the best cars for your needs.
www.eta.co.uk

Look up the official figures for the carbon dioxide emissions of cars on the market in the UK here:
www.vcacarfueldata.org.uk

US fuel-economy figures are available from the government here:
www.fueleconomy.gov

The Greener Cars website in the USA has information on fuel economy and tips for greener driving.
www.greenercars.org

Look up crash-test scores for cars on sale in Europe at the Euro NCAP website.
www.euroncap.com

Information about greener cars and alternative fuel vehicles available in the UK, including electric motorbikes, is brought together at the Green Car Site.
www.greencarsite.co.uk

Find out about the G-Wiz electric city car here:
www.goingreen.co.uk

SCHOOL TRAVEL

The Safe Routes to School website gives advice on walking and cycling to school, and how to set up a walking bus.
www.saferoutestoschools.org.uk

Bikeability is the new cycling award scheme for children in the UK, with online advice and activities for kids and parents.
www.bikeability.org.uk

The Walking Bus website offers professional advice and support for your walking bus.
www.walkingbus.org

Many Forestry Commission sites offer active educational days out for schools.
www.forestry.gov.uk

School parties are welcomed at many of the Wildlife Trusts' nature reserves. Find your local sites on their website.
www.wildlifetrusts.org

WORK TRAVEL

The Car Share website contains a directory of hundreds of local car-sharing projects and services around the country. You and your colleagues could join an existing scheme or use the advice of other local schemes to start your own.
www.carshare.com

The Department for Transport has a comprehensive guide available online to help employers set up and implement a workplace travel plan.
www.dft.gov.uk

The Energy Saving Trust gives advice to organisations and businesses on workplace travel plans and greener business travel.
www.energysavingtrust.org.uk/fleet

Bus Users UK can help you or your employer to set up a local bus-users group or to press local bus companies for better services to cover your workplace.
www.bususers.org

LONG-DISTANCE TRAVEL

Look up UK rail timetables and buy tickets online here:
www.thetrainline.com

There isn't a central ticket and information service for UK express coaches online, but these companies all have wide coverage of the country:

National Express
www.nationalexpress.com

Scottish Citylink
www.citylink.co.uk

Megabus
www.megabus.com

Here are some places to book European international rail tickets:
www.europeanrail.com
www.raileurope.co.uk
www.railbookers.com

And some places to book coaches in Europe:
www.eurolines-travel.com
www.busabout.com
www.berlinlinienbus.de

GREENER HOLIDAYS

The Man in Seat Sixty-One has a wealth of advice and detailed information on booking non-flying travel tickets all over the world, including details of Motorail trains across Europe.
www.seat61.com

Enjoy England, the official tourist board for England, has information for every area of the country, and links to local tourist boards.
www.enjoyengland.com

The website for Scotland's national tourist board has lots of information on things to see and do in Scotland.
www.visitscotland.com

Wales has some amazing unspoilt sites. Find out more at its tourism website.
www.visitwales.co.uk

The British Trust for Conservation Volunteers offers working holidays doing conservation work around the UK.
www2.btcv.org.uk

Or, for a lazier, but still unique, holiday close to home, stay in one of the Landmark Trust's historic buildings.
www.landmarktrust.org.uk

TRAVEL BETTER WHEN YOU FLY

Cheatneutral is a spoof website with a hilarious demolition of offsetting as a very poor solution to flying's carbon emissions. www.cheatneutral.com

The Clean Development Mechanism's Gold Standard validation system, based in Switzerland and supported by a range of environmental organisations, is the only organisation in the world that is validating carbon-offsetting projects that truly bring extra carbon savings. So far, very few projects have been validated and brought into operation, but the site does list offsetting companies that are using its registered carbon credits on this page: www.cdmgoldstandard.org/background.php?id=50

The International Voluntary Service has hundreds of volunteering and conservation projects you can take part in all over the world. www.ivs-gb.org.uk

Coral Cay Conservation expeditions involve taking part in scientific conservation work, surveying and protecting coral reefs and tropical forests.
www.coralcay.org

Voluntary Service Overseas needs skilled professionals to spend up to two years abroad working alongside people in developing countries.
www.vso.org.uk

Hotelbook is a worldwide online booking service that only includes independent hotels.
www.hotelbook.com

Europe and Relax features bed-and-breakfast accommodation across Europe.
www.europeandrelax.com

For greener hotels, look at Conservation International's eco-tourism information service.
www.ecotour.org

Responsible Travel is an agency that recognises the need to cut down on flying, seeks out greener holidays all over the world, and campaigns for more responsible tourism.
www.responsibletravel.com

Leabharlanna Poibli Chathair Bhaile Átha Cliath
Dublin City Public Libraries